DISCARD

D1567934

OCT 15

WHAT HAPPENED AT
AREA 51?

By Barbara M. Linde

Gareth Stevens
PUBLISHING

Please visit our website, www.garethstevens.com. For a free color catalog of all our high-quality books, call toll free 1-800-542-2595 or fax 1-877-542-2596.

Library of Congress Cataloging-in-Publication Data

Linde, Barbara M., author.
  What happened at Area 51? / Barbara M. Linde.
    pages cm. — (History's mysteries)
  Includes bibliographical references and index.
  ISBN 978-1-4824-2102-6 (pbk.)
  ISBN 978-1-4824-2101-9 (6 pack)
  ISBN 978-1-4824-2103-3 (library binding)
  1. Unidentified flying objects—Sightings and encounters—Nevada—Juvenile literature.
  2. Conspiracies—United States—History—20th century—Juvenile literature. 3. Air bases—Nevada—Juvenile literature. 4. Research aircraft—Juvenile literature. 5. Area 51 (Nev.)—Juvenile literature. I. Title. II. Series: History's mysteries (New York, N.Y.)
  TL789.2.L56 2015
  001.942—dc23
                                                      2014035344

First Edition

Published in 2015 by
Gareth Stevens Publishing
111 East 14th Street, Suite 349
New York, NY 10003

Copyright © 2015 Gareth Stevens Publishing

Designer: Katelyn E. Reynolds
Editor: Therese Shea

Photo credits: Cover, pp. 1, 20 photoBeard/Shutterstock.com; cover, pp. 1–32 (background texture) Kevin Kay/Shutterstock.com; p. 5 SipaPhoto/Shutterstock.com; p. 7 DigitalGlobe/Getty Images; p. 8 NASA/Wikipedia.com; p. 9 Carl Mydans/The LIFE Picture Collection/Getty Images; p. 10 US Air Force/Wikipedia.com; p. 11 USAF Museum/Wikipedia.com; p. 13 (illustrations) Newresid stephanelhernault@yahoo.fr/ Wikipedia.com; p. 13 (photo) USGOV-PD/Wikipedia.com; p. 15 Chris Parypa Photography/Shutterstock.com; p. 17 NASA; p. 18 schmaelterphoto/Shutterstock.com; p. 19 (*Independence Day*) Kim Kulish/AFP/Getty Images; p. 19 (*Close Encounters of the Third Kind*) Columbia Pictures/Getty Images; p. 21 (sign) MWaits/Shutterstock.com; p. 21 (newspaper) drew peacock/Wikipedia.com; p. 22 Cooper.ch/Wikipedia.com; p. 23 Rob Boudteau/The Image Bank/Getty Images; p. 25 (document) CIA (Richard Helms)/Wikipedia.com; p. 25 (Groom Lake) Doc Searls/Wikipedia.com; p. 27 (Ronald Reagan) Paul Shambroom/Science Source/Getty Images; p. 27 (Barack Obama) Saul Loeb-Pool/Getty Images; p. 29 Finlay McWalter/Wikipedia.com.

Printed in the United States of America

CPSIA compliance information: Batch #CW15GS: For further information contact Gareth Stevens, New York, New York at 1-800-542-2595.

CONTENTS

A Mystery in the Desert 4

The History of Area 51 6

Spy Planes 8

Enemy Planes 12

Working at Area 51 14

Conspiracy Theories 16

UFO Headquarters 22

Declassified Documents 24

Presidential Talk 26

Mystery: Solved or Unsolved? 28

Glossary 30

For More Information 31

Index 32

Words in the glossary appear in **bold** type
the first time they are used in the text.

A MYSTERY
IN THE DESERT

Picture this. You're near Las Vegas, Nevada. You know there's a military base in the desert. Sometimes you see shiny metallic **discs** flying high in the sky. At night, weird glowing lights float down and land somewhere.

You've been told that several unmarked airplanes take off and land at the nearby Las Vegas airport every day. The people who board those planes never discuss their work. A dirt road winds through the remote area. Signs warn you to keep out, but you've seen plain, white buses loaded with people traveling that road.

You're near Area 51. It's a real place. Some of the stories about it are true. Others are hard to confirm. You can make up your own mind about them.

REVEALED!

"UFO" stands for "unidentified flying object." Not all UFOs are of alien origin. It's just a way of saying the aircraft hasn't been recognized yet.

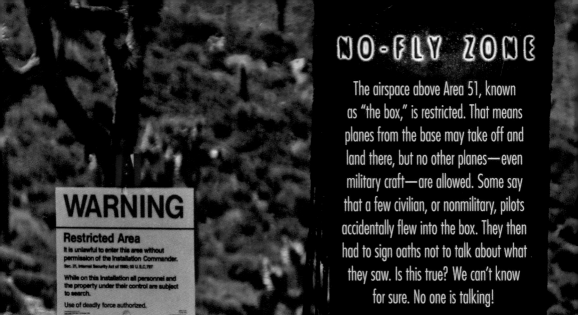

NO-FLY ZONE

The airspace above Area 51, known as "the box," is restricted. That means planes from the base may take off and land there, but no other planes—even military craft—are allowed. Some say that a few civilian, or nonmilitary, pilots accidentally flew into the box. They then had to sign oaths not to talk about what they saw. Is this true? We can't know for sure. No one is talking!

WARNING

Restricted Area

It is unlawful to enter this area without permission of the Installation Commander.
Sec. 21, Internal Security Act of 1950; 50 U.S.C. 797

While on this installation all personnel and the property under their control are subject to search.

Use of deadly force authorized.

WARNING!

NO TRESPASSING
AUTHORITY N.R.S. 207-200
MAXIMUM PUNISHMENT: $1000 FINE
SIX MONTHS IMPRISMENT
OR BOTH
STRICTLY ENFORCED

PHOTOGRAPHY OF THIS AREA IS PROHIBITED

18 USC 795

WARNING

MILITARY INSTALLATION

IT IS UNLAWFUL TO ENTER THIS INSTALLATION WITHOUT THE WRITTEN PERMISSION OF THE INSTALLATION COMMANDER.

INSTALLATION COMMANDER
AUTHORITY: Internal Security Act, 50
U.S.C. 797
PUNISHMENT: Up to one year imprisonment and $5,000. fine.

These warning signs are posted at Area 51, just off the main road. Why are they necessary? What's going on there?

THE HISTORY OF
AREA 51

Area 51 is a plot of land that borders now-dry Groom Lake in Nevada, just outside the Nevada Test and Training Range, where nuclear testing once took place. The term "Area 51" probably came from maps from the 1950s that labeled the areas around Groom Lake.

During World War II (1939–1945), the US Army used Area 51 as a training ground. In the early 1950s, the CIA (Central Intelligence Agency) began working with Lockheed, an aircraft manufacturer. They needed a secret facility to develop and test **surveillance** aircraft. The former army site was just right.

At the time, the United States and the Soviet Union were involved in the **Cold War**. The United States wanted planes that could secretly fly into Soviet airspace and photograph its military operations.

REVEALED!

In 2000, photographs of Area 51 taken by the Soviets were obtained by American scientists. The Soviets had been taking pictures of the secret base since the 1960s!

OTHER NAMES

Originally, Area 51 was referred to as Paradise Ranch, or just the Ranch, to sound appealing to workers. In 1956, the CIA named it Watertown after Watertown, New York, the birthplace of CIA director Allen Dulles. In the late 1970s, the air force renamed it Detachment 3, Air Force Flight Test Center. It's also been called Dreamland, Home Base, the Test Site, Home Plate, and G-Base. Now, its official name is National **Classified** Test Facility.

This is a **satellite** view of Area 51. Today, we know Area 51's exact location is latitude 37 degrees 14 minutes north, longitude 115 degrees 48 minutes west.

SPY PLANES

In 1954, Project Aquatone was established to develop the spy plane that would be known as the U-2. Everyone involved in the research at Area 51 was sworn to secrecy. Pilots and mechanics didn't even know all the facts. Only a few officials had the whole picture.

The unusual-looking, shiny aluminum U-2 flew at 70,000 feet (21,336 m) and reached speeds of 500 miles (805 km) per hour. Pilots wore specially made pressurized suits. They looked quite odd—even alien! The test flights often lasted several hours and traveled almost all the way across the country.

Secret U-2 flights and UFO rumors started around the same time. People reported seeing strange shapes and lights in the night sky. The government's cover story was that they were flying weather-observation planes.

REVEALED!
Special cameras on the U-2 photographed enemy military bases and equipment.

the U-2

U-2 SHOT DOWN

On May 1, 1960, a U-2 piloted by Francis Gary Powers was shot down over the Soviet Union. Powers landed the plane safely, but was captured. The incident caused great tension between the United States and the Soviet Union. Powers was sentenced to 10 years in a Soviet prison for **espionage**, but returned home after he was exchanged for a Soviet prisoner in 1962. There are still many questions surrounding the downing of the U-2, such as how Soviet weapons could have reached such a height.

Francis Gary Powers died in 1977. The military gave his family awards owed to Powers for his secret work, including a Distinguished Flying Cross, a Department of Defense Prisoner of War Medal, and a National Defense Service Medal.

In 1962, Project Oxcart produced the A-12, which was made of strong, shiny **titanium**.

This **stealth** plane reached 90,000 feet (27,432 m) at speeds of 2,300 miles (3,700 km) per hour. It could fly coast-to-coast in about 70 minutes! Its disc-shaped body, along with unheard-of speed and height, added to the UFO rumors. The government stuck to the story of weather-observation planes. The famous **reconnaissance** plane SR-71 Blackbird was developed from the A-12.

Have you heard of any of these other stealth planes tested at Area 51?

- Have Blue (1977): the first model for the F117-A bomber
- Tacit Blue (1982): designed to fly low for reconnaissance
- Bird of Prey (1996): believed to be able to camouflage itself

Tacit Blue

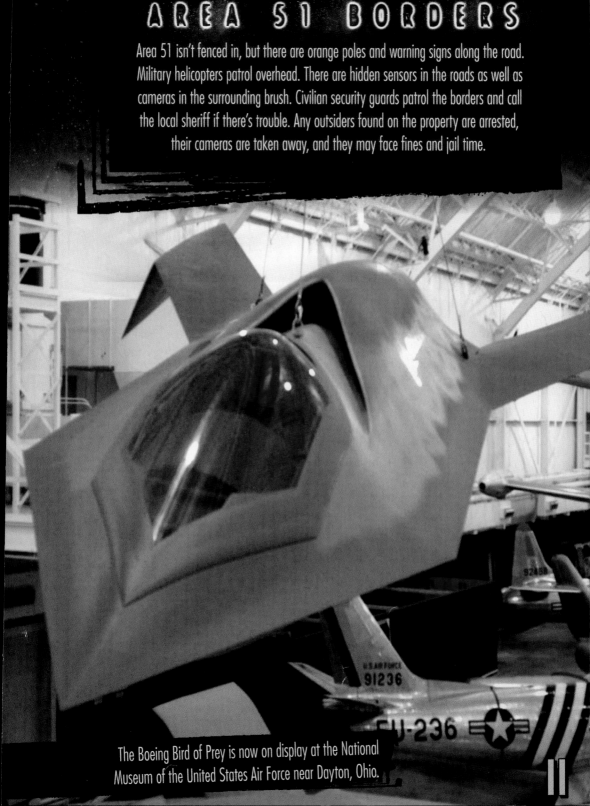

AREA 51 BORDERS

Area 51 isn't fenced in, but there are orange poles and warning signs along the road. Military helicopters patrol overhead. There are hidden sensors in the roads as well as cameras in the surrounding brush. Civilian security guards patrol the borders and call the local sheriff if there's trouble. Any outsiders found on the property are arrested, their cameras are taken away, and they may face fines and jail time.

The Boeing Bird of Prey is now on display at the National Museum of the United States Air Force near Dayton, Ohio.

ENEMY PLANES

In 1967, the United States received a captured Soviet MiG-21F jet fighter. The plane was taken to Area 51. The secret project to learn more about the Soviet aircraft was named "Have Doughnut." Skilled mechanics used a process called reverse engineering to find out more about it. They took apart the plane, studied the parts, and then put the jet back together. After that, test pilots flew it in pretend battles with American fighter jets.

In 1969, two projects called "Have Drill" and "Have Ferry" began at Area 51. These involved MiG-17F planes obtained from Syria. By the mid-1980s, the United States had several additional Soviet aircraft to study. This work gave the US military valuable information about the capabilities of its enemies. Engineers then made improvements on US military planes.

REVEALED!

When the Soviets discovered one of their planes was at Area 51, they positioned spy satellites overhead. To trick the Soviets, engineers painted fake aircraft shapes on the runways.

BREAKTHROUGHS

Area 51 engineers also worked with captured Soviet radar systems. Their studies helped create new stealth **technology**. At the same time, the American fighter pilots who flew the MiGs started training US Navy pilots. This was the start of the navy's Top Gun training program. The training helped American pilots face MiG planes flown by the North Vietnamese during the Vietnam War (1959–1975).

CCCP 1962

Vietnam 1967

Bulgaria 1963

MiG-21 F-13
"FISHBED C"

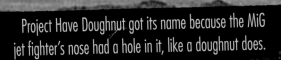

Project Have Doughnut got its name because the MiG jet fighter's nose had a hole in it, like a doughnut does.

13

WORKING AT
AREA 51

Area 51 is in a remote location in the desert. So how do workers get there? The process has been the same since the beginning. They commute by bus and airplane. Unmarked planes use special buildings at the Las Vegas airport. The planes all identify themselves to the airport as "Janet" followed by a number. The passengers then get on a bus and are driven to Area 51.

Area 51 workers wear casual clothes, not business suits, military uniforms, or anything that would give clues about their work or positions. They sign national security oaths to never talk about what they see or do. Workers often have to stay inside buildings that don't have windows when test flights are going on outside.

REVEALED!

The secrecy and timing of the "Janet" flights may be responsible for some UFO sightings, too.

PROBLEMS FOR WORKERS

Some former Area 51 workers say the government burned toxic wastes there. There's also **radiation** from nuclear tests at Area 51 and the nearby test and training range. Workers and even nearby residents have become ill or died, perhaps because of this. Workers fought the government who said, at first, that Area 51 didn't have to follow the same laws as other military bases. Finally, though, the government agreed to clean up the site.

Workers commute on Boeing 737-200 "Janet" planes.

CONSPIRACY THEORIES

There are several **conspiracy theories** related to Area 51. Let's take a look at some of them.

On July 20, 1969, astronauts Neil Armstrong and Buzz Aldrin became the first men to walk on the moon. This amazing feat generated national pride—and a conspiracy theory. A UFO magazine article said that an alien spacecraft was on the moon when the astronauts arrived. Similar stories followed, but NASA (National Aeronautics and Space Administration) ignored them. Then, in 1974, a man named William Kaysing published a book stating the moon landings were faked, later adding they were filmed at Area 51.

Interestingly, NASA astronauts really did visit Nevada. That's because the land around Area 51 is harsh, rocky terrain a lot like the lunar surface.

REVEALED!

During a TV interview, Buzz Aldrin said, "Conspiracy theories are a waste of everybody's time and energy."

KAYSING DEBUNKED

Kaysing's Conspiracy Theories	The Truth
The American flag was fluttering on the windless moon.	The flag had a special frame that made it appear to wave.
There aren't any stars in the photographs.	Sunlight reflected off the moon's surface. The astronauts' camera wasn't powerful enough to photograph the stars.
The Eagle lander didn't create a crater beneath it.	There's no air on the moon, so there wasn't enough pressure to create a crater.

Do you think this photograph shows Neil Armstrong on the moon—or at an Area 51 film set?

Does an underground tunnel system connect Area 51 with other military bases

around the country? Some people think so. They say a train runs through the tunnels—all the way to the East Coast! If World War III ever happens, government officials would be able to escape to safety in the tunnels and use the trains.

While some say there are no such tunnels at Area 51, there are definitely tunnels under the nearby Nevada testing site. These are used for research and secret projects. Trains carry equipment and workers through the tunnels. The widespread system probably started the rumors about Area 51. However, there's no proof of a maze of tunnels stretching from coast to coast.

Area 51

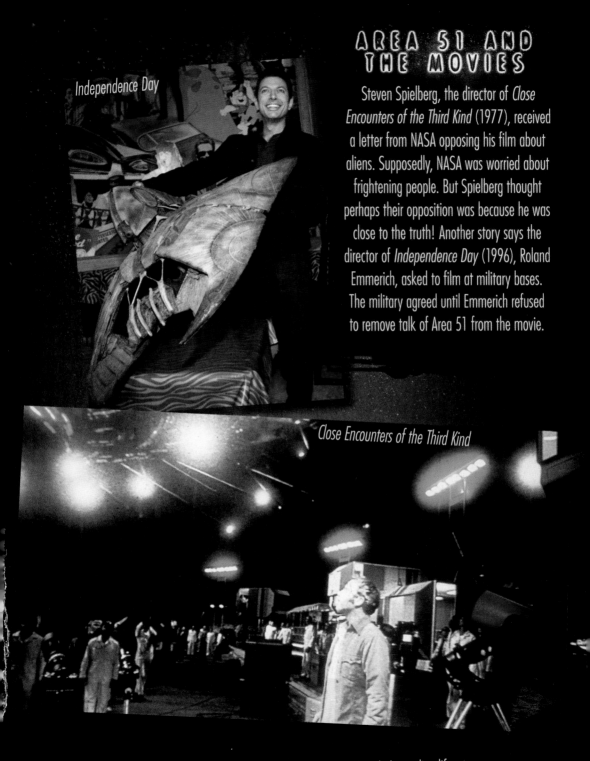

AREA 51 AND THE MOVIES

Independence Day

Steven Spielberg, the director of *Close Encounters of the Third Kind* (1977), received a letter from NASA opposing his film about aliens. Supposedly, NASA was worried about frightening people. But Spielberg thought perhaps their opposition was because he was close to the truth! Another story says the director of *Independence Day* (1996), Roland Emmerich, asked to film at military bases. The military agreed until Emmerich refused to remove talk of Area 51 from the movie.

Close Encounters of the Third Kind

People's fascination with aliens is reflected in the many movies produced about alien life.

In early July 1947, a rancher near Roswell, New Mexico, found unusual looking debris from a crashed aircraft. At first, the army said the vehicle was a UFO. Soon after, they said it was a weather balloon. They classified all information about the event, though. Some people think the debris was moved to Area 51.

In 1989, a man named Bob Lazar shocked the nation when he came forward saying he had worked on alien spacecraft at Area 51. Lazar claims he reverse engineered alien ships. He also reported that much of our advanced technology comes from alien spacecraft. However, the government denies he ever worked for them. Lazar no longer comments about Area 51.

REVEALED!

Some say alien bodies were recovered along with the aircraft in Roswell!

model of an alien

WHY "FLYING SAUCERS"?

On June 24, 1947, a pilot in Washington reported seeing a group of nine disc-shaped aircraft flying at incredible speeds. He said they looked like they were saucers skipping over water. So, the press called these objects "flying saucers." The incident has been forgotten by many, but the name "flying saucer" stuck. Many UFOs are called flying saucers despite their varying shapes.

This was the front page of the local newspaper reporting on the crashed aircraft in Roswell in 1947. "RAAF" stands for "Roswell Army Air Field."

UFO HEADQUARTERS

The tiny town of Rachel, Nevada, is a perfect distance for observing nearby Area 51. Perhaps for that reason, it's become known as the "UFO Capital of the World." People gather on the hillsides, hoping to catch glimpses of alien spacecraft hovering near the base. The "Keep Out" signs and patrolling guards only further their suspicions and interest.

The town's motel, the Little A'Le'Inn, began selling alien-themed T-shirts and other items. Then the owners started a "UFO Friendship Campout" for tourists to gather and watch for spacecraft. Bob Lazar even spoke at one of the gatherings in 1993.

However, most area residents believe that the bright lights at night are "Janet" flights and test planes. They say the loud booms are from military aircraft—not aliens.

REVEALED!

A minor league professional baseball team in Las Vegas is called the Las Vegas 51s.

THE BLACK MAILBOX

Bob Lazar said he told people to meet him at a black mailbox on Highway 375 to see test flights of alien spacecraft. The site became a destination for UFO hunters, much to the annoyance of the rancher who owns the mailbox. He finally painted the mailbox white. He has said many times that he doesn't believe the aircraft flying overhead are alien in origin. Still, it's a popular site for tourists even today.

Extraterrestrial Highway

NEVADA 375

©1996 STATE OF NEVADA. All Rights Reserved.

The state of Nevada renamed Highway 375 "Extraterrestrial Highway."

DECLASSIFIED
DOCUMENTS

In 2013, the government declassified, or
ade public, over 60 documents, mostly from the
)60s and 1970s. These papers describe the Area
l stealth programs and reverse engineering of the
iGs. They're available for anyone to read online,
it they may disappoint UFO fans: They don't
ention aliens or alien spaceships.

In 1974, astronauts on Skylab, a US space
ation circling Earth, accidentally captured an
nage of the Groom Lake area, including Area
l. Area 51 was the only place Skylab astronauts
eren't supposed to photograph. When the error
as discovered, the photo was kept from public
ew. The photo was declassified with the other
)cuments in 2013.

The government says it wasn't trying to
de anything from its citizens. Instead, it was
ncerned with keeping
nportant information
vay from enemy
overnments.

REVEALED!

NASA thought the Skylab photo
should be released to the public. The
Department of Defense disagreed.

II. OXCART RECONNAISSANCE OPERATIONS PLAN

1. The required photographic coverage of North
will be accomplished by the OXCART vehicle operating
Kadena Air Base in Okinawa. This operating location
has been prepared for OXCART operation for some time

2. Operational missions will be planned, direc
controlled by the Central Intelligence Agency Opera
Center. Three OXCART aircraft and the necessary ta
personnel will be deployed from Area 51 to Kadena.

3. With this inventory a minimum of nine (9)
operational missions per month can be flown consis
available weather. Overcast skies are a predomin
associated with the monsoon season and limit the
suitable for effective photographic reconnaissanc
monsoon season wanes, the number of clear days in
permitting more frequent, repetitive reconnaissan
Missions will be launched on a twenty-four hour alert basis.
This will permit maximum utilization of the favorable weather
available. In addition to the operational missions flown,
necessary test and proficiency sorties will be flown from Kadena.
OXCART aircraft will be rotated [   ] to
maintain the required number of operationally ready aircraft at

THE BLACK BUDGET

The US government has a secret budget for classified programs called the "black budget." It's so secret that not even all members of Congress know where or how the money is spent. We do know that the CIA receives more than one-fourth of the total—about $14.7 billion in 2013! The public is definitely in the dark about where the money goes, but we can guess that a lot of the money goes to programs at Area 51.

Groom Lake is a salt flat, an area where salt has been left behind after water has evaporated. It's used as a runway. A declassified document is shown above left.

PRESIDENTIAL TALK

During the 2013 Kennedy Center Honors, President Barack Obama became the first US president to mention Area 51 by name. He joked, when he first became president, "one of the questions that people ask you is 'What's really going on at Area 51?' " He later added, "I think I just became the first president to ever publicly mention Area 51." President Obama didn't reveal any of the work that goes on there, though, just like the presidents before him.

Presidents George W. Bush and Bill Clinton also referred to Area 51, but only in writing. And they never mentioned it by that name. Instead, they called it "the United States Air Force's operating location near Groom Lake, Nevada."

REVEALED!

In 1955, President Dwight D. Eisenhower approved of the establishment of Area 51, according to now-declassified documents.

PRESIDENTIAL UFO!

In 1974, President Ronald Reagan told a reporter that he had seen a UFO while flying in a plane: "We followed it for several minutes. It was a bright white light. We followed it to Bakersfield [California], and all of a sudden to our utter amazement it went straight up into the heavens." Suddenly, Reagan seemed to remember that he was speaking to a reporter and became quiet. He never talked of the event again.

Ronald Reagan

Barack Obama

Will future presidents reveal more information about the activities at Area 51?

MYSTERY: SOLVED OR UNSOLVED?

According to the US Air Force, the mission of Area 51 is "the testing of technologies and systems training for operations critical to the effectiveness of US military forces and the security of the United States." When interviewed for a National Geographic video, some of the early test pilots would only say that it was an honor to serve their country. They believe that some secrets are necessary to protect the country. And now, over 50 years later, they still keep those secrets.

Area 51 has grown in the years since it began. Work continues, and the projects that take place there are still highly classified. What kinds of planes are being built and tested? What other operations are going on? Are there aliens and alien spacecraft? We may never know the answers to our most burning questions.

REVEALED!

Now that Area 51 is the "worst kept" secret in the United States, some people think the government is building another superclassified base.

There's one way you can find out what's happening at Area 51. You could work there. Take a lot of math, science, and computer technology courses in school. When you're older, you could work for a company like JT3, which hires civilians for many government projects at the Nevada Test Site. You could also join the US Air Force and become a test pilot. Who knows what kind of amazing plane you'll fly—or what alien spacecraft you'll encounter!

MAP OF AREA 51

It's not a secret where Area 51 is, but getting onto the base is still nearly impossible for civilians.

GLOSSARY

classified: made available only to certain people for reasons of national security

Cold War: the nonviolent conflict between the United States and the Union of Soviet Socialist Republics (USSR) during the second half of the 20th century

conspiracy theory: a belief that an event is the result of a secret plot by powerful people rather than what it appears to be

disc: an object that is thin, flat, and circular

espionage: the use of spying to gather secret information

radiation: harmful energy in the form of tiny particles

reconnaissance: the exploration of a place to collect information

satellite: an object that circles Earth in order to collect and send information or aid in communication

stealth: the act of doing something quietly and secretly

surveillance: the act of watching someone or something closely

technology: the way people do something using tools and the tools that they use

teleportation: the theory of moving matter from place to place without traveling through a physical space

 titanium: a strong, lightweight, silvery metallic element

FOR MORE INFORMATION

BOOKS

Martin, Ted. *Area 51*. Minneapolis, MN: Bellwether Media 2012.

Meltzer, Brad, with Keith Ferrell. *History Decoded: Solving the Ten Greatest Conspiracies of All Time*. New York, NY: Workman Publishing Company, 2013.

WEBSITES

Area 51 Declassified Facts
channel.nationalgeographic.com/articles/area-51-declassified-facts/
Read the facts about Area 51 and its secrets.

The Area 51 File: Secret Aircraft and Soviet MiGs
www2.gwu.edu/~nsarchiv/NSAEBB/NSAEBB443/
Read the recently declassified government documents about Area 51.

How Area 51 Works
science.howstuffworks.com/space/aliens-ufos/area-51.htm
Learn the history of Area 51 and find out about the mysteries that surround it.

INDEX

A-12 10

aliens 4, 8, 16, 19, 20, 22, 23, 24, 28, 29

"box, the" 5

conspiracy theories 16, 17

cover story 8, 10

declassified documents 24, 25, 26

Groom Lake 6, 24, 25, 26

"Janet" flights 14, 15, 22

Kaysing, William 16, 17

Las Vegas, Nevada 4, 14, 22

Lazar, Bob 20, 22, 23

MiGs 12, 13, 24

moon landing 16, 17

movies 19

Nevada Test and Training Range 6, 15, 18, 29

nuclear tests 6, 15

Project Aquatone 8

Project Oxcart 10

Rachel, Nevada 22

reverse engineering 12, 20, 24

Roswell, New Mexico 20, 21

stealth planes 10

stealth technology 13, 24

teleportation 18

test flights 6, 8, 10, 12, 14, 22, 23, 28, 29

time travel 18

toxic wastes 15

U-2 8, 9

UFO 4, 8, 10, 14, 16, 20, 21, 22, 23, 24, 27

underground tunnel system 18

weather control 18